She Reins

She Reins

Head up, Heels Down.

WILLOW CREEK PRESS

Published by Willow Creek Press, Inc.
P.O. Box 147, Minocqua, Wisconsin 54548

Photo Credits:

Printed in China

It's hard to fail but its worse
never to have tried to succeed.

Some of my best friends
never say a word to me.

Of all the paths you take in life
make sure a few of them are dirt.

Kind heart,
fierce mind,
brave spirit.

If you have gained the trust of a horse,
you have won a friend for life.

Surely, of all the
wonders of the world,
the horizon is the greatest.

Don't follow the path,
blaze the trail.

Let a horse whisper in your ear
and breathe on your heart.
You will never regret it.

Only those
who dare,
truly live.

Courage is like a muscle.
We strengthen it by use.

She would rather
walk alone in darkness
than follow anyone else's shadow.

Nothing is so strong as gentleness

Nothing so gentle as real strength.

It does not matter
how slowly you go,
so long as you
do not stop.

Sometimes you can't see yourself clearly until you see yourself through the eyes of others.

A pony is a childhood dream;
a horse is an adult treasure.

Rise above the storm and you will find sunshine.

Be a girl with a mind,
a woman with attitude,
and a lady with class.

All I need is the sound of hooves
beneath me and the sky above me.

If you are too busy to laugh, you are too busy.

Today walk with courage
in all you do.

GARDENING

Everyone shines given the right lighting

Some women fear the fire.
Some women simply become it.

Beautiful creatures cannot be confined.
Her wings will grow, she'll find the sky.

A sweet friendship refreshes the soul.

"You're gonna be happy" said life,
"but first I'll make you strong."

The horse is a mirror to your soul.
Sometimes you might not like what you see.
Sometimes you will.

Where there is a woman
there is magic.

Head up,
heels down.

Our greatest experiences
are our quiet moments.

Courage is being scared to death
but saddling up anyway.

Horses
lend us
the wings
we lack.

Of all the roads she traveled
the journey back to herself
was the most magnificent.

A good rider can hear
his horse speak to him.
A great rider can hear
his horse whisper.

The wind of heaven is that which
blows through a horse's ears.

Feeling down?
Saddle up.

I am who I truly am,

when I am in the saddle.

There is peaceful.

There is wild.

I am both at the same time.

Without hard work,
nothing grows but weeds.

She conquered
her demons
and wore her
scars like
wings.

She beats to the beauty
of her wildflower heart
and seashore soul.

In riding a horse
we borrow freedom.

She will rise. With a spine of steel and a roar like thunder, she will rise.

I live in a house,
but my home is in the stable.

It is the horse's gift
to connect us with
Heaven and our own footsteps.